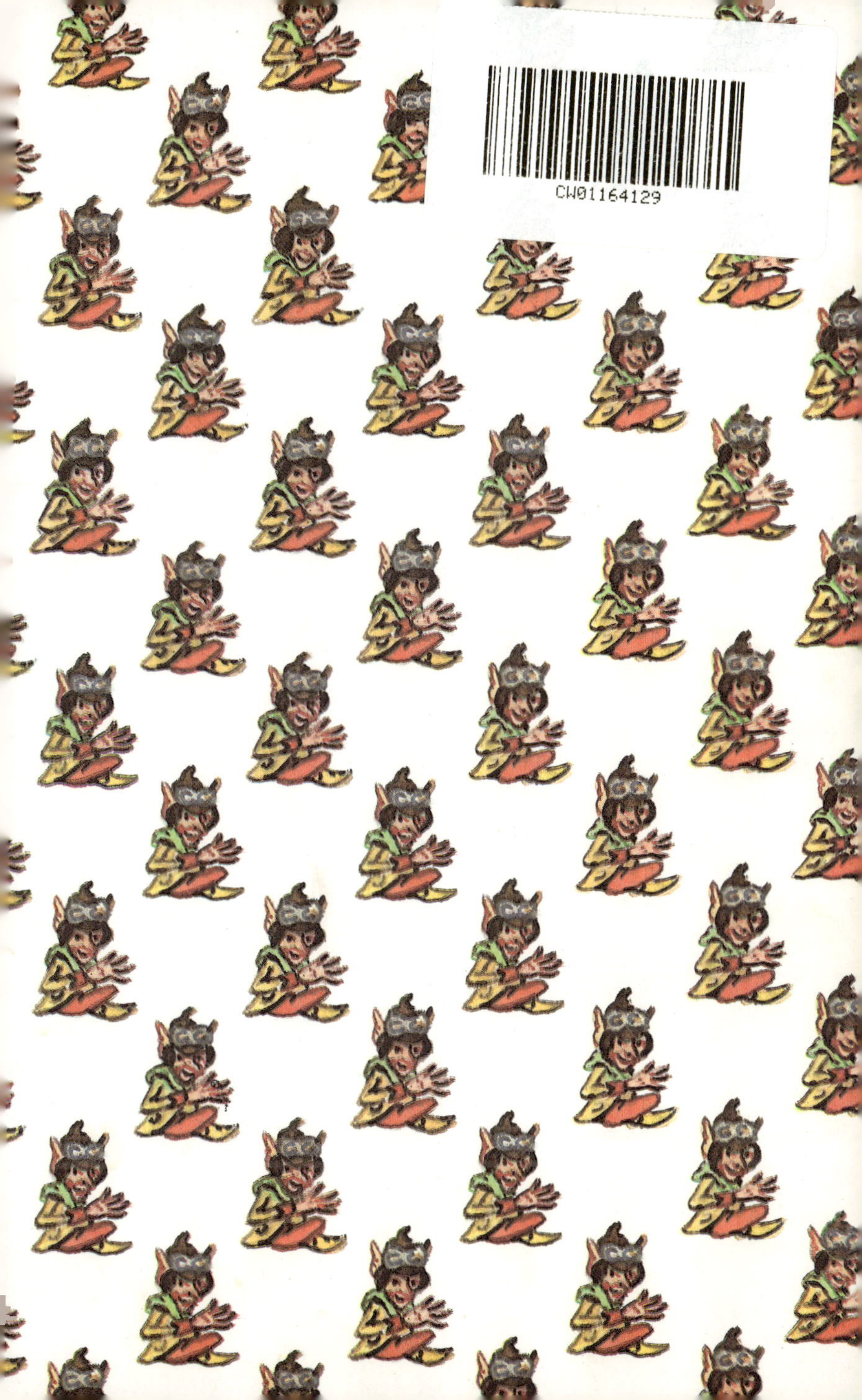

A CAT IN FAIRYLAND AND OTHER TALES

A Cat in Fairyland
The Very Little Hen
The Brave Little Puppy (previously The Very Brave Puppy)

Copyright © Darrell Waters Limited 1949
Copyright © illustrations Century Hutchinson Limited 1986
First published by Pitkin London 1949

Published in 1986 by Hutchinson Children's Books
An imprint of Century Hutchinson Ltd
Brookmount House, 62–65 Chandos Place, Covent Garden,
London WC2N 4NW

Century Hutchinson Publishing Group (Australia) Pty Ltd
16–22 Church Street, Hawthorn, Melbourne, Victoria 3122

Century Hutchinson Group (NZ) Ltd
32–34 View Road, PO Box 40–086, Glenfield, Auckland 10

Century Hutchinson Group (SA) Pty Ltd
PO Box 337, Bergvlei 2012, South Africa

Designed by Sarah Harwood
Edited by Sarah Ware

Set in Souvenir Light 774 12/14pt.
by Southern Positives and Negatives (SPAN), Lingfield, Surrey

Printed and bound in Italy

British Library Cataloguing in Publication Data

Blyton, Enid
    A cat in fairyland and other tales.
    I. Title   II. Hook, Richard
    823'.912[J]   PZ7

ISBN 0 09 167210 4

Enid Blyton's
A CAT IN FAIRYLAND
and other tales

Illustrated by

Francis Scholes

Hutchinson
London Melbourne Auckland Johannesburg

A CAT IN FAIRYLAND

BIMBO was a big black cat, the finest puss in the town. His whiskers were four inches long, his tail was fat and furry. His coat shone like silk, and his purr was so loud that it sounded like a motorbike out in the road!

He belonged to Jenny and Simon, and they loved him very much.

'He is the most beautiful puss I've ever seen,' said Jenny.

'If only he could talk, it would be lovely,' said Simon. 'He's so clever he could teach us a lot.'

Bimbo often used to go out for walks with Jenny and Simon. When they took their tea to Hallo Wood, Bimbo ran behind them, sat down with them, and shared their milk. Then he would go prowling off by himself, not very far away, always keeping the children well in sight.

One day all three started off, their tea in a basket. They went right to the middle of Hallo Wood, sat down and began their tea. When they had finished Bimbo stalked off on his own, as usual. And suddenly a very strange thing happened.

Jenny happened to look up from the book she was reading and saw a strange little man, rather like a gnome, walking quietly through the trees. On his back he carried a large empty sack. Jenny nudged Simon and both children stared at the gnome in surprise and excitement, for they

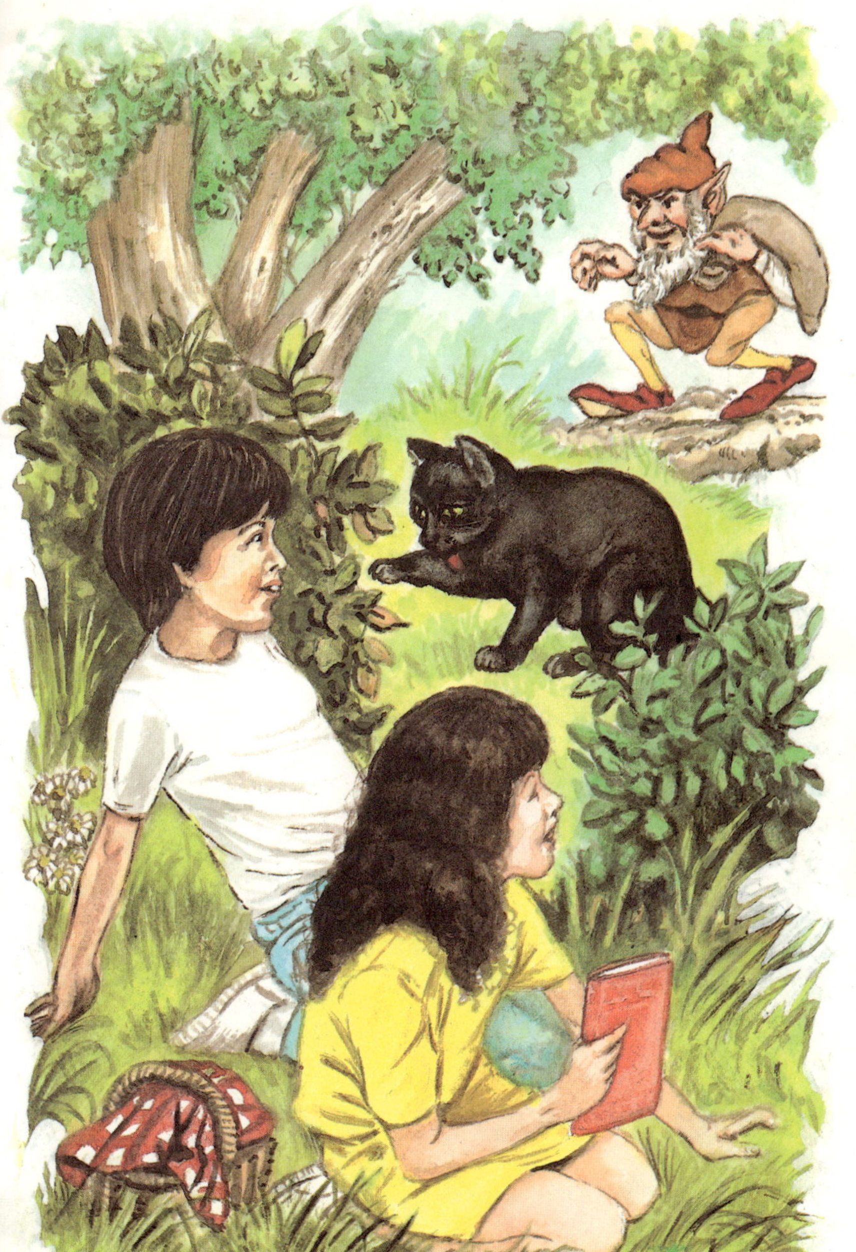

A CAT IN FAIRYLAND

had never seen any kind of fairy before.

Bimbo didn't see the gnome. He was sitting down, washing himself, purring very loudly. The gnome crept up behind him, opened his large sack, and suddenly flung it right over Bimbo.

Jenny and Simon jumped up at once, shouting angrily. The gnome turned and saw them. At once he pulled the mouth of the bag tight, threw it over his shoulder with poor Bimbo struggling inside, and ran off through the wood. Jenny and Simon followed, fearful and raging, wondering what the gnome wanted with their beautiful cat.

Panting and puffing the gnome tore through the wood, with Jenny and Simon after him. He ran into a thick bush, and when the children came up, he had disappeared. They couldn't see him anywhere.

'Oh, poor Bimbo!' said Jenny, almost crying. 'Where has he been taken to? Oh, Simon, we really must find him and rescue him.'

'Well, I don't see where the gnome has gone to,' said Simon, puzzled. He looked round and ran here and there, but there was no sign of the gnome.

'We'd better go home and tell Mummy,' he said. 'Come on.'

But they had lost their way! They couldn't find the path they had taken in following the gnome, and they were quite lost. Jenny began to feel frightened, and wondered if the gnome would come back and take them prisoner too, but Simon cheered her up, and said that he would fight a dozen gnomes if he could see them.

'There's a little path running along here,' he said to Jenny. 'We'd better follow it. It must lead somewhere.'

So they ran down it, and after some time they came to the prettiest little cottage they had ever seen, so small that it really didn't look much more than a large doll's house.

Simon knocked at the yellow front door, and a pixie with silvery wings opened it. She looked so surprised to see them.

'We've lost our way,' said Simon, politely. 'Could you please help us?'

'Come in,' said the pixie. 'Mind your heads.'

They had to stoop down to go inside, for the door was so small. Inside the cottage were small chairs and a tiny table. It was the funniest little place. Jenny was half afraid of sitting down in case she broke the chair she sat on.

'Let me offer you a cup of tea,' said the pixie, and she hurried to her small fireplace and took a boiling kettle off the hob.

'Well, we've really had tea,' said Simon, 'but it would be nice to have a cup of pixie tea, so thank you very much, we will.'

Then while the pixie made sweet-smelling tea in a little flowery teapot, and set out tiny currant cakes, Simon and Jenny told her all about the gnome who had stolen Bimbo, their cat.

'Now did you ever hear such a thing!' said the pixie, in surprise. 'I'm sure I know where your puss has been taken.'

'Oh where?' asked the children at once.

'To the old wizard, Too-Tall,' said the pixie, handing the plate of buns to Jenny. 'I know that his last cat, who used to help him in his spells, ran away a little while ago, and he has been wanting another. That gnome you saw is his servant, and I expect he has been looking out for a good black cat. When he saw your Bimbo he captured him at once, and I expect he took him straight to his master, Too-Tall.'

'But Bimbo would hate to help anyone with spells,' said Jenny. 'He's just an ordinary cat, and he would be very unhappy to live away from us. The wizard has no right to take him!'

'Could we rescue him, do you think?' asked Simon. 'Where does this wizard live?'

A CAT IN FAIRYLAND

'He lives in Runaway House, not very far from here,' said the pixie.

'What a funny name!' said the children.

'Well, it's a funny house,' said the pixie. 'It's got four little legs underneath it, and when the wizard wants to move, he just tells it to run where he wants it to, and the legs run away at once, taking the house with them.'

'Goodness me!' said Jenny, her eyes shining with excitement. 'Wouldn't I like to see it!'

'I'll take you there, if you like,' said the pixie, and she wrapped a little coat round her. 'But mind – don't make a noise when we get there, or the old wizard might put a spell on us.'

'Will we be able to rescue Bimbo, do you think?' asked Simon.

'We'll see when we get there,' said the pixie, opening the front door. 'Come along.'

She took them back to the thick bush where the gnome had disappeared. To the children's surprise they saw a little trap door hidden under the bush. The pixie pulled it open, and all three of them climbed down some steps into an underground passage. Then for some way they walked in darkness, guided only by the pixie's voice in front of them. Soon a little lamp shone out, and Jenny and Simon saw a crowd of little doors in front of them.

The pixie opened a blue one and led the way into a small room, where a grey rabbit was writing at a desk. He looked up, and asked where they wanted to go.

'To Runaway House,' answered the pixie. The rabbit gave them each a green ticket, and told them to sit on three little toadstools in the corner. They all sat down and the rabbit pressed a button. In a trice the three toadstools shot upwards and Jenny and Simon clutched at the edges in surprise.

For a long time they went up and up, and at last the toadstools slowed down. They came to a stop inside another small room, where a second rabbit sat. He took their tickets, opened a door and showed them out into the sunshine.

A CAT IN FAIRYLAND

'What an adventure!' said Simon, who was thoroughly enjoying himself. 'I did like riding on those toadstools!'

They were on a hillside, and the pixie pointed to a little house at the top, surrounded on three sides by trees, to shelter it from the wind.

'That's Runaway House,' she said. 'You can see the feet peeping from underneath it. When it runs it raises itself on its legs and goes off like lightning!'

The three made their way up to it, and the pixie tiptoed to a little window at the back. She peeped inside, and beckoned to the children. They crept up and looked in.

Bimbo was inside! He sat on the floor in the middle of a chalk ring, looking very angry and very miserable. His great tail swept the floor from side to side and his fine whiskers twitched angrily.

The wizard Too-Tall, a thin bent old man in a pointed hat, was standing opposite the cat, waving a long stick. He looked very cross. In a corner by the fireplace was the gnome who had stolen Bimbo, stirring something in a big pot.

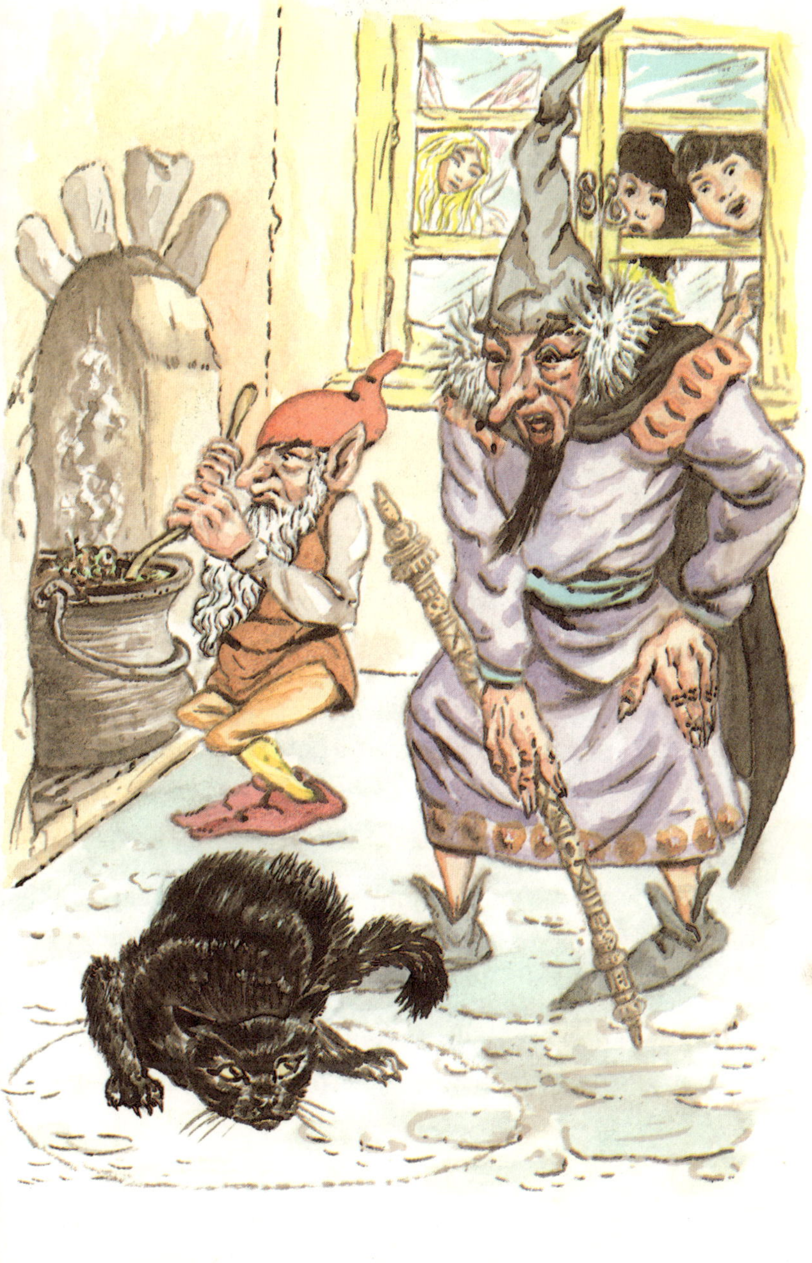

A CAT IN FAIRYLAND

'You must help me with my magic spells, or I will turn you into a mouse!' said the wizard to Bimbo. And then to the children's enormous surprise, Bimbo opened his mouth and spoke.

'Are your spells all good ones?' he asked. 'For I tell you this, Master Wizard, no cat belonging to my honourable family would ever help in making a bad spell for witches or goblins to use!'

'I am not a good wizard,' said Too-Tall, with a horrid smile. 'I make my money by selling magic to witches, and if you are too grand to help me, my honourable cat, I shall have to do as I said, and turn you into a mouse. Then you will be hunted by your honourable family, and be punished for your stupidity.'

Poor Bimbo began to tremble, but he still would not agree to help Too-Tall, and the wizard grew impatient.

'I will give you one more chance,' he said at last. 'Unless you stand up on your hind legs, turn round twice and mew seven times loudly whilst I chant my magic words and wave my enchanted stick, you shall be changed into a little brown mouse!'

A CAT IN FAIRYLAND

He began to wave his long stick and chant curious words, which made the little pixie outside shiver and shake. But Bimbo did not stand up and mew as he had been told. He sat there in the middle of the ring, looking very much frightened, but quite determined not to help the wicked old wizard.

Then Too-Tall lost his patience. He struck Bimbo with his stick, called out a magic word, and then laughed loudly – for the black cat suddenly vanished, and in its place cowered a tiny brown mouse.

'Now you see what your punishment is!' cried the wizard. 'Go, hide yourself away, miserable creature, and be sure that when I get another cat, you will be hunted for your life!'

A CAT IN FAIRYLAND

The little mouse rushed away into a corner, and hid itself in an old slipper. Jenny and Simon could hardly believe their eyes when they saw that their lovely Bimbo had vanished, and in his place was a poor little mouse.

Jenny began to cry, but Simon doubled up his fists, half inclined to go in and fight the wizard and gnome.

'Don't do anything foolish,' whispered the pixie, dragging the two away from the window. 'Hush, Jenny, don't cry, or the wizard will hear you, and he might quite easily change all of us into mice too.'

'But I must do something about poor Bimbo,' said Simon, fiercely.

'Well, I've got a plan,' said the pixie. 'Listen. We'll wait till darkness comes, and then borrow three spades from Tippy, an elf who lives near by. We'll dig a big hole just a little way down the hill. Then we'll all borrow trays and trumpets, and make a fearful noise outside the cottage.

A CAT IN FAIRYLAND

The wizard will wake in a fright and think a great army is marching against him. He will order his house to run away, and as the only way it can run is down the hill because there are trees on every other side, it will fall straight into the pit we have dug for it!'

'What then?' asked the children in excitement, thinking it was a marvellous plan.

'Well, I'll pop inside the house before the wizard has got over his fright, and get his enchanted stick,' said the pixie, delightedly. 'He's no good without that, you know. You, Simon, must get hold of the gnome and hold him tightly. You, Jenny, must pick up the little mouse. The wizard will probably run away, for he is an awful coward without his magic stick.'

'Go on, go on!' cried the children, their eyes shining.

'That's all,' said the pixie. 'We'll just run off to Tippy's, then, and I'll see what I can do about Bimbo for you.'

Night was coming on, for the sun had gone down over the hill. The pixie led the way to a large toadstool on the other side of the hill. It had a little door in it and the pixie knocked. An elf opened the door, and peeped out.

'Who is it?' he asked.

'It's only Tuffy the Pixie,' said the pixie. 'Can you lend us three spades, Tippy?'

'Certainly,' said Tippy, and he took three little spades from a corner of his strange toadstool house. The pixie took them, said thank you, and ran off again with the children. They passed the wizard's house, which was now lighted inside by a swinging lamp, and went a little way down the hillside.

Then they began to dig. How they dug! The pixie said a little spell over their spades to make them work quickly, and the hole soon began to grow. The spades flew in and out, and the children got quite out of breath.

At last it was finished. The moon shone out in the sky, and the pixie said they had better wait for a big cloud to come before they carried out the next part of their plan, for if the house could see before it as it ran, it would run round the hole they had made, instead of into it.

'I'll take the spades back to Tippy's and borrow a few trays and things,' whispered the pixie. 'You stay here, and watch to see that everything is all right.'

It wasn't long before the pixie was back again. She had with her three trays, two trumpets and a large whistle. She giggled as she handed out the things to the children.

A CAT IN FAIRYLAND

'What a shock the wizard will get!' she said. 'Now creep with me just outside the cottage, and when I say 'GO!' bang on your trays and blow your trumpets hard. I'll blow my whistle, and if we don't give the wizard the fright of his life, I shall be surprised!'

They all crept up to the cottage. 'GO!' suddenly shouted the pixie as soon as a cloud came over the moon. In a trice there was a most fearful noise! The trays clanged, the trumpets blared, the whistle blew, and in between all three shouted at the top of their voices.

A CAT IN FAIRYLAND

The wizard was sitting at his table eating his supper with the gnome. When they heard the fearful din outside, the wizard leapt to his feet and turned very pale.

'It's the elfin army after us!' he shouted. 'House, house, find your feet, run away, fast and fleet!'

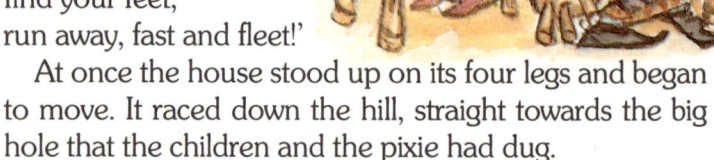

At once the house stood up on its four legs and began to move. It raced down the hill, straight towards the big hole that the children and the pixie had dug.

A CAT IN FAIRYLAND

Plonk! It fell right into it. Chimneys flew about, windows smashed, and the wizard and the gnome cried out in terror. They couldn't get out of the door because it was buried in the pit, so they tried to get out of the window.

'Come on!' cried the pixie. 'Into the house, all of you!'

Jenny and Simon rushed to the fallen house. They climbed in at one window, and the pixie climbed in at another. Jenny ran to the corner where she saw the frightened little mouse peeping out of a slipper. She picked it up and slipped it into her pocket.

A CAT IN FAIRYLAND

Simon rushed at the gnome and held him tightly, then called to Jenny to tie him up with a piece of rope he saw lying by the fire. The pixie snatched up the wizard's enchanted stick with a cry of delight.

The old wizard had scrambled out of his window and was rushing down the hill in the moonlight. He was frightened out of his wits!

'Leave the gnome and come away now,' said the pixie. 'If that old wizard meets any witch he knows he may bring her back here, and that would be awkward.'

The three climbed out of the tumbled-down house and ran down the hillside to give back the trays, trumpets and whistle. As they came back again, the pixie pointed to the east with a shout of dismay.

'There's the wizard with two witches! Come on, we shall have to hurry.'

She took the children to the door that led to the toadstool room where the rabbit sat. In a twinkling they had their tickets and were sitting on three toadstools. Just as the strange lifts had started to rush downwards the wizard and witches came racing into the room, and sat down on other toadstools.

'Ooh, my, now we're in for a race!' groaned the pixie. 'Jump off your toadstools as soon as they stop and run for the door. Race down the passage and up the steps to the trap door as fast as ever you can!'

So as soon as the toadstools stopped, Jenny and Simon leapt off them, ran to the door, and raced into the passage as fast as their legs would take them. The pixie followed, and even as they all reached the door they saw the wizard and witches landing in the room on their toadstools.

They tore along the passage and up the steps, with the wizard and witches after them. When they got outside they banged the trap door down, but the wizard pushed it open almost at once. Then the pixie gave a shout of triumph.

'What a silly I am! I'd forgotten I'd got Too-Tall's enchanted stick!' she cried. 'I'll soon settle him!'

She waited till Too-Tall and the witches had climbed out of the trap door, and then she danced towards them, waving her stick and chanting a long string of words.

The wizard gave a howl of fright, and raced back to the trap door. The witches followed, and soon there was a bang as the trap door closed.

'They're gone, and they won't come back in a hurry!' said the pixie, in delight. 'What a good thing I remembered I had Too-Tall's stick. I can use it on Bimbo too, and change him back from a mouse to a cat.'

They all hurried to the pixie's cottage. She drew a circle of chalk on the floor, put the frightened mouse in the middle, waved the enchanted stick and cried out a magic word. Immediately the mouse vanished, and in its place appeared Bimbo, the big black cat!

Bimbo gave a loud purr and leapt over to the delighted children. What a fuss he made of them! They stroked him and loved him and he rubbed his big head against them.

'Now what about a hot cup of cocoa and a slice of cake?' asked the pixie. 'It's quite time you went home, you know, or your mother will be very worried about you.'

So they all sat down to hot cocoa and slices of ginger-cake. Then the pixie showed them the way home through the wood. She shook hands with them, stroked Bimbo and said good-bye.

A CAT IN FAIRYLAND

'Good-bye' said Jenny and Simon, 'and thank you ever so much for helping us. We only wish we could do something in return for your kindness.'

'Don't forget I've got the wizard's magic stick!' said the little pixie with a laugh. 'I never in all my life expected to have such a wonderful thing as that! That's quite enough reward for me! Now good-bye to you both, and run home quickly.'

Off went Jenny, Simon and Bimbo, and very soon they ran up the path to their house. Mummy was looking for them, and was getting very anxious. When she heard their story she looked most astonished.

'What an extraordinary thing!' she cried. 'I can hardly believe it, my dears.'

'Well, Mummy, we'll get Bimbo to guide us to the pixie's cottage in Hallo Wood tomorrow,' said Jenny. So the next day they told Bimbo to take them there – but wasn't it a pity, he couldn't remember the way!

'Perhaps he will one day,' said Simon. 'We must wait for that.'

And as far as I know, they are still waiting.

THE VERY LITTLE HEN

THERE was once a fine fat hen called Chucky, who laid beautiful brown eggs every single day. She belonged to Dame See-Saw, and was one of a big flock, for the old dame made her living by selling eggs.

Now one day Chucky wandered out of the old woman's garden. She knew she ought not to do this, for she had often been warned that the world outside was not good for hens. But the gate was open and out she walked.

She hadn't gone very far before she met Ten-Toes the pixie.

'Good morning,' he said. 'Come here, my dear, and let me see what sort of an egg you can lay me for my dinner. I'm very hungry indeed, and a nice boiled egg would do me a lot of good!'

So Chucky laid him an egg. It was one of her very best, big and brown, and Ten-Toes was very pleased. He made himself a fire, put his little saucepan on to boil, and very soon the egg was in the bubbling water. Ten-Toes ate it with a crust of bread, and said that it was the nicest he had ever tasted.

'You must come home with me,' he said to Chucky. 'I'd like an egg like that every day.'

'Oh, I can't come with you,' said Chucky, frightened. 'I belong to Dame See-Saw. I must go back.'

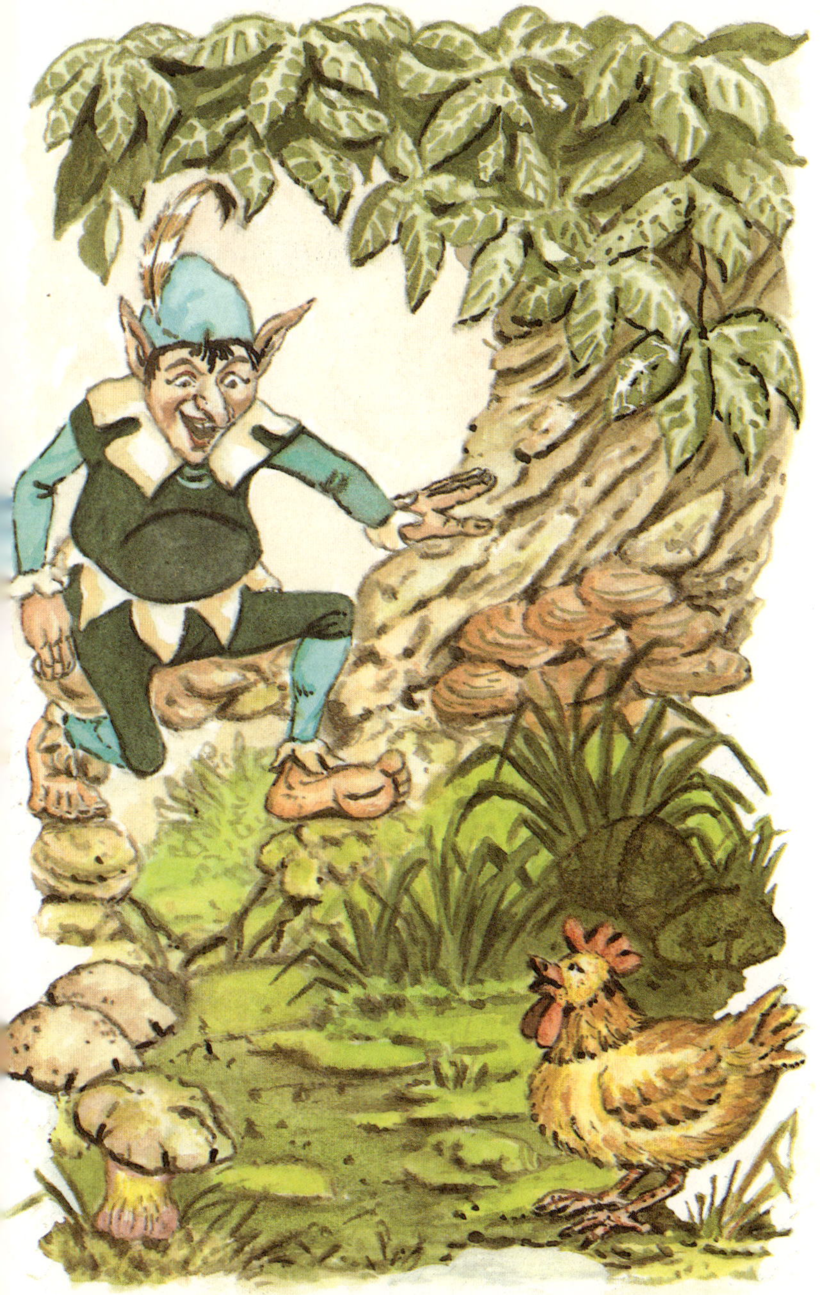

'No, no,' said Ten-Toes, and he picked up the fat brown hen. But she struggled so hard, and pecked his finger so badly that he grew angry.

'Ho ho!' he said, in a nasty voice. 'So you think you won't come with me, do you? Well, I'll soon show you that you're wrong.'

With that he tapped Chucky on the head with his wand and said two magic words. In a trice the hen grew much, much smaller – so small that she was no bigger than a buttercup flower!

'Ha!' said Ten-Toes. 'Now you can peck all you like, but you won't be able to hurt me! And when I get you home, I'll change you back to your right size again, and make you lay me an egg every day!'

But when Chucky heard that, she fled off between the blades of grass, clucking loudly in fear. At first she didn't know what had happened to her, but soon she guessed that she had been made very, very small, for the grass towered above her, and the face of a daisy seemed as big as the sun!

THE VERY LITTLE HEN

She made her way back to Dame See-Saw and told her all that had happened.

But Dame See-Saw was cross. 'What use are you to me now, I'd like to know?' she cried. 'I can't turn you back to your right size again, and all the other hens will peck you. The eggs you lay will be so tiny that I shan't be able to sell them. You can just walk out of the garden gate again, and go to seek your living somewhere else!'

Poor Chucky! She ran out of the gate, clucking in despair. Who would have her, now that she was so small?

THE VERY LITTLE HEN

'I'll go to Tweedle the Gnome,' she thought. 'He isn't very big. Perhaps he'd like to keep me.'

But Tweedle laughed when he saw Chucky.

'What good would your eggs be to me?' he asked. 'Why, I could put twenty in my mouth at once and not know they were there! No, I don't want you, Chucky.'

Then the little hen went to the goblins in the hill, though she was really rather afraid of them. But they didn't like eggs.

'We never eat them,' they said. 'And we couldn't sell them, Chucky, because they are so very tiny. No, we don't want you, Chucky.'

Chucky wandered off to the Wise Man, and begged him to keep her, and she would lay him eggs every day.

'But what could I do with them?' asked the Wise Man. 'They're so small that I should have to put on my biggest pair of spectacles to see them. No, Chucky, I don't want you!'

Poor Chucky went away sadly. Nobody wanted her. There wasn't any room for her anywhere. She went on and on until at last she came to a beautiful garden. In one corner of it was built a play-house for the children, and in this they kept all their toys.

There was a rocking-horse, a big shelf full of books, a toy fort, a Noah's ark, two dolls, a toy clown, a teddy-bear, a box of tricks and last of all, a lovely toy farm. The little hen peeped in at the door and thought it was a fine place. She wondered if there was anyone there who would like to have her for their own.

But Peter and Jane, who owned the lovely play-house, were not there. They were staying at their Granny's, so the toys were all alone. They saw the tiny hen at the door and called to her to come in.

'What a little mite!' they cried. 'Are you alive or are you a toy like us?'

'I'm alive,' said Chucky, and she told the toys her story, and how she could find nowhere to live. Then the toys all began to talk at once, and there was a tremendous noise. At last the teddy-bear held up his hand for silence, and everyone was still.

'Chucky,' said the teddy-bear to the tiny hen, 'would you like to come and live with us here? There is a toy farm over there, with sheep, cows, horses, goats, pigs, ducks and one cock. There used to be a hen, too, but she got broken. The cock that is left is lonely, and as he is just about your size, we are sure he would be delighted to welcome you to his little shed.'

Chucky was so happy that she could hardly speak. She looked at the little toy farm and thought it was the prettiest place she had ever seen. It was all fenced round, and the farm stood in the middle with the barns and sheds here and there. The farmer and his wife, both made of wood, waved to Chucky.

THE VERY LITTLE HEN

She ran to them, and they bent down and stroked her. She was just the right size for them. Then the little wooden cock strutted up, and admired Chucky. His feathers were only painted on, but Chucky's were real, and he thought she was wonderful.

'Welcome to my shed!' he said, and he led Chucky to the door of a tiny shed near by.

'I think I'll lay the farmer an egg to show how grateful I am,' said Chucky, and she straightaway laid a beautiful brown egg in the little nesting box there. How delighted the farmer and his wife were! All the toys crowded round to see it, too!

'Well, the other hen that got broken never laid an egg in her life!' cried the farmer's wife. 'What a clever little thing you are, to be sure!'

'Lets have some baby chickens!' cried the farmer. 'We won't eat your eggs yet, Chucky. Lay a dozen in the nesting box, and then sit on them. It would be grand to have twelve yellow chicks running about the farm!'

So Chucky laid twelve brown eggs, and sat on them – and do you know, one morning they all hatched out into the tiniest, prettiest yellow chicks you ever saw! Chucky and everyone else were so proud of them! It made the toy farm seem quite real, to have the little chicks running about everywhere.

Tomorrow Peter and Jane are coming back from their Granny's – and whatever will they say when they see the little chicks, each no bigger than a pea, racing about the toy farm, cheeping loudly? I really can't think!

As for Chucky, she has quite forgotten what it was like to be a great big hen. She is happy as the day is long, trotting about with her chicks on the little toy farm.

THE BRAVE LITTLE PUPPY

ONE day, when Martin and Clare were walking home from school, they saw a man throw a little puppy into a pond, and then run off and leave it.

'Oh!' cried Clare in a rage. 'Look, he's tied a brick round the poor little thing's neck, Martin, and he meant to drown it. Quick! Let's get it out!'

Martin took off his shoes and socks, waded into the pond and picked up the struggling puppy. He quickly undid the string that tied the brick round its neck, and then carried the shivering little creature back to the bank.

'Let's take it home, and see if Mummy will let us keep it,' said Clare. 'Poor little thing! What a horrid man that was!'

They carried the puppy home – but, oh dear, Mummy wouldn't let them have it.

'No,' she said, 'you have two rabbits and a kitten and that's quite enough. You can't have a puppy too. Besides, it is a very ugly little thing.'

'But what shall we do with it?' asked Clare.

'Daddy's got to go to town this afternoon and he'll take it to the Dog's Home,' said Mummy. 'It will be looked after there until somone comes and offers to give it a good home. You had better go with Daddy into town, too, and have your hair cut, both of you.'

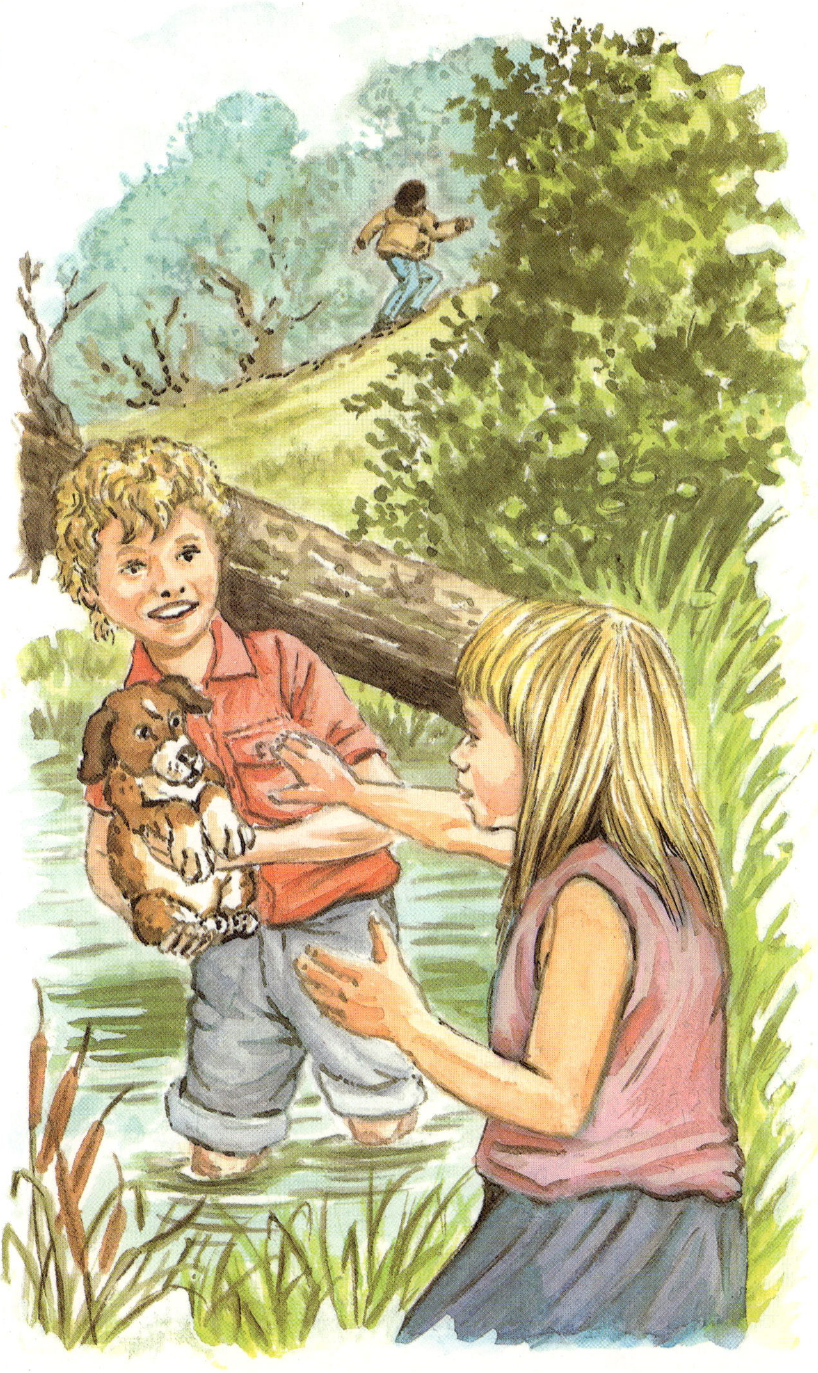

So that afternoon Daddy and the two children got into a little brown car and drove off to town. Clare carried the puppy, which wriggled and licked her happily, thinking it had found a lovely master and mistress at last. The children thought it was the nicest little puppy they had ever seen, and even Daddy said it wasn't a bad little thing when it had licked the back of his ear a dozen times.

'Here's the hairdresser's,' said Daddy, pulling up by the kerb. 'Come on, you two. Leave the puppy in the car, and we'll all go and have our hair cut.'

So into the shop they went, leaving the puppy in the car. Soon all three were sitting in chairs with big white cloths round them, and snip, snip, snip went the scissors.

THE BRAVE LITTLE PUPPY

Outside the shop were two men. They had seen Daddy and the children go into the hairdresser's and they knew that it would be some time before they came out again.

'Let's take this car, Bill,' said one the men. 'We can jump into it and drive off before anyone stops us!'

'But isn't that a dog inside?' said the other man.

'Pooh, that's only a puppy!' said the first man. 'Come on, quick, before a policeman comes!'

He opened the car door, and at the same moment the puppy started barking his very loudest, for he knew quite well that the two men were not the kind children, nor their father. The man cuffed the puppy, and he bared his little white teeth and snarled. He was very much afraid of this nasty rough man, but the car was in his charge, and he was going to guard it as best he could.

THE BRAVE LITTLE PUPPY

So he flew at the man who was trying to sit in the driver's seat, and bit him in the arm with all his might. The man tore him away and flung him into the back of the car, but, still barking, the brave little dog once more hurled himself at the thief.

Then Martin and Clare heard him barking, and Martin ran to the window and looked out.

'Daddy, Daddy!' he cried, 'There're two men trying to take the car! Quick! Quick! The puppy is trying to stop them, but they'll soon be away!'

Daddy rushed out of the shop at once, followed by the hairdresser and another man. In a trice they had captured the two thieves and the hairdresser went to telephone the police. In a few minutes the bad men were marched off to the police station, and Daddy and the children went back to have their hair finished.

'Well, that puppy is about the bravest little thing I *ever* saw!' said Daddy. 'I've a good mind to keep him, after this. He stopped our car from being stolen, there's no doubt of that. What about taking him home again, children, and telling Mummy what he's done? Perhaps she would let you keep him then.'

THE BRAVE LITTLE PUPPY

'Oh, Daddy!' cried Martin and Clare in delight. 'Do let's!'

So they all drove home again with the puppy, and Daddy told Mummy how his bravery had saved their car from being stolen. The puppy looked at Mummy with his brown eyes, and wagged his stumpy tail hopefully.

'Well, we'll keep him!' said Mummy. 'I'm sure he will grow up into a very brave, faithful dog. You shall have him, children.'

So that is how Pickles the puppy came to belong to Martin and Clare. He is a grown-up dog now, and twice he has scared away burglars, and once he pulled Baby out of the water when she fell in. Mummy is very glad she let Martin and Clare keep him – and of course they think he is the very best dog in all the world!

THE ENID BLYTON TRUST FOR CHILDREN

We hope you have enjoyed these stories. Please think for a moment about those children who are too ill to do the exciting things you and your friends do.

Help them by sending a donation, large or small, to the ENID BLYTON TRUST FOR CHILDREN. The trust will use all your gifts to help children who are sick or handicapped and need to be made happy and comfortable.

Please send your postal orders or cheques to:

The Enid Blyton Trust for Children
International House
1 St Katharine's Way
London E1 9UN

Thank you very much for your help

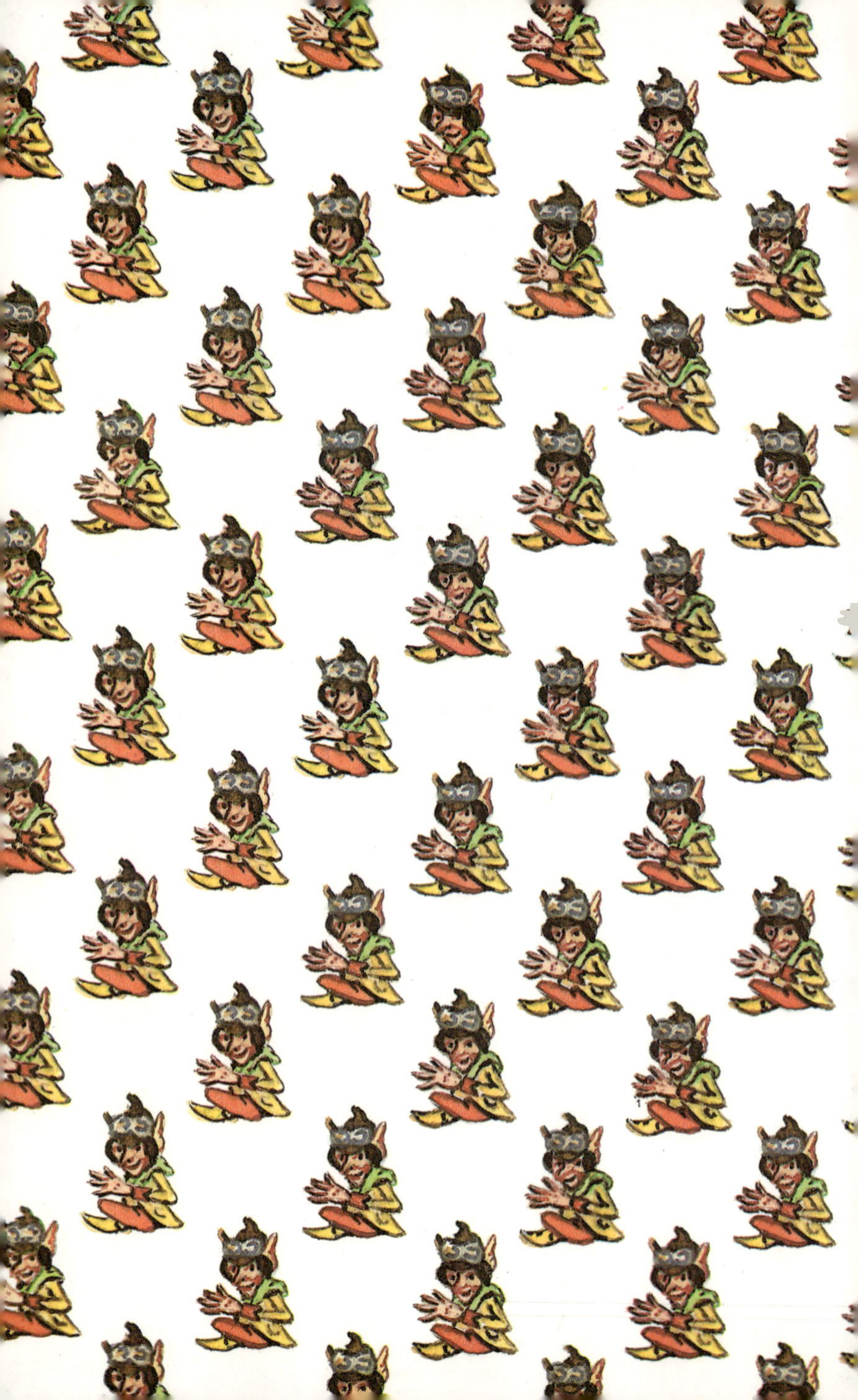